Steve Jobs and Apple

INTERNET BIOGRAPHIES

Steve Jobs and
Apple

THERESE SHEA

ROSEN PUBLISHING®

New York

Published in 2013 by The Rosen Publishing Group, Inc.
29 East 21st Street, New York, NY 10010

First Edition

Library of Congress Cataloging-in-Publication Data

Shea, Therese.
Steve Jobs and Apple/Therese Shea.—1st ed.
    p. cm.—(Internet biographies)
Includes bibliographical references and index.
ISBN 978-1-4488-6910-7 (library binding)
1. Jobs, Steve, 1955–2011. 2. Businesspeople—United States—Biography. 3. Apple Computer, Inc. 4. Computer industry—United States. 5. Computer engineers—United States—Biography. I. Title.
HD9696.2.U62J639 2012
338.7'6100416092—dc23
[B]

2011040098

Manufactured in the United States of America

CPSIA Compliance Information: Batch #S12YA: For further information, contact Rosen Publishing, New York, New York, at 1-800-237-9932.

Contents

INTRODUCTION

Wire-rimmed glasses, black turtleneck, and jeans—this was the iconic outfit that Steve Jobs wore whenever he stepped out into the public eye. Jobs, the co-founder of Apple, was never an ingenious engineer, nor was he the most talented designer. His greatest gift was the ability to know what technology the public wanted, even before they did. He was able to bring out the best in his brightest employees to make this technology a reality. Perhaps most important, his undeniable charisma helped him attain the status of one of the world's most admired business leaders.

To understand Jobs's appeal in the technology world, one only needed to attend the unveiling of an Apple product. The most anticipated moment of the day was when Jobs stepped out onto the stage as the master of ceremonies. Several thousand Apple fans greeted him as enthusiastically as any rock star and quickly hushed when he began to speak. Jobs kept them enthralled while introducing the newest Apple offering. He freely wove words such as "brilliant" and "landmark" into his addresses. When Jobs talked about his long-term vision for the company, his passion became contagious. He both inspired and made people laugh. His personality was so ingrained in

Steve Jobs enthusiastically explains several innovative Apple products, including the iPod Mini, at an unveiling in San Francisco, California, in 2004.

the culture of his company that his keynote speech was often called the "Stevenote" speech. Apple stock prices were known to spike after his addresses. Similarly, after Jobs's announcement in August 2011 that he was stepping down as chief executive officer (CEO) due to health problems, shares of the company plunged.

Jobs was so connected to the popularity of Apple, it is easy to forget that there were several years when he was not a part of it. He credited this time of professional struggle for his success, calling it the best thing that could have happened to him. His ventures NeXT Inc. and Pixar Animation Studios were part of this period and are important pieces of his story. Jobs even found the humor in his hard times, describing the loss of a quarter of a billion dollars in one year as "very character-building," according to author Owen Linzmayer. But his great conviction for innovation, coupled with his commanding leadership, placed him back on top of the business world. Even in an economic recession, Apple rose to become the most valuable company in the United States in August 2011, with its stock price even surpassing that of oil giant ExxonMobil for a time. Apple's creations have become ubiquitous, and yet each year's new models entice consumers with better features.

Sadly, Jobs died on October 5, 2011, at the age of fifty-six. Celebrities, dignitaries, business leaders, and the multitudes of people who loved Apple products all mourned his death. Facebook, Twitter, and other online forums buzzed with condolences. So many people felt Jobs had touched their lives that Apple's board of directors observed, "The world is immeasurably better because of Steve."

What kind of businessman can evoke this kind of passion? What qualities did Jobs embody that earned him such heartfelt praise yet raised an empire of technology? Certainly his ambition played a part, but that alone was not enough for him to succeed. He learned many lessons through his experiences during the early years of Apple, in the halls of his company NeXT, and in the studio with the Pixar animation team. He learned about trust, innovation, and adaptation in the business world. The result is an unparalleled success story.

CHAPTER 1

Childhood: Apple's Seeds

S teve Jobs's life could have been much different. Were it not for a difficult decision made by his birth mother, he might have grown up in a different part of the country, or he might have pursued a different career. Most certainly, he would not have been "Steve Jobs."

He was born on February 24, 1955, in San Francisco, California. His mother was a young, unmarried graduate student. After anguishing about her baby's future, she decided to give up the child for adoption. The young woman wanted her baby boy to have a certain kind of life, and she believed his adoptive parents had to be college graduates to give him this life. The first couple interested in adopting the baby was a lawyer and his wife. However, at the last minute, they decided they wanted a little girl instead. Late one night, a couple named Paul and Clara Jobs received one of the most important phone calls of their lives.

Steve's Other Family

Steve Jobs did not know who his birth mother was while growing up. In the 1980s, he hired a private detective to find out her identity. Joanne Simpson (formerly Schieble) was her name. When Jobs met her, she told him that his father was a man named Abdulfattah Jandali. The two had attended the University of Wisconsin together. After the adoption, they married and had another child, a girl named Mona. The couple split up several years later. His mother then moved and remarried. After Jobs met her and his biological sister, he developed a warm relationship with both of them. Mona Simpson is a successful novelist for whom Jobs publicly expressed his admiration.

Though he rarely talked about his adoption, Jobs was always grateful that he ended up with Paul and Clara Jobs, whom he referred to as his "real parents."

An adoption agency with which they were registered called to see if they were interested in adopting a little boy. They were overjoyed. They had been waiting hopefully to adopt a child for some time. But there was a problem—neither Clara nor Paul had graduated from college. In every other way, they were perfect candidates. Paul was a machinist. Though he had never completed high school, he had served in the U.S. Coast Guard during World War II. Clara, a payroll clerk, had not finished college.

For a few months, Steve's mother would not sign the adoption papers. Paul and Clara offered a guarantee that made her change her mind: they promised the baby boy would go to college. Finally, his mother agreed to the adoption, and soon Clara and Paul took home Steven Paul Jobs.

SILICON VALLEY

When Steve was five, Paul Jobs got a new job. The family—now larger with the adoption of Paul and Clara's daughter, Patti—moved from San Francisco to Mountain View, California. This area, the Santa Clara Valley, is now known as Silicon Valley because it is the heart of the U.S. technology industry. (Silicon chips, manufactured in the area, were a major development in the evolution of computers.) When the Jobs family relocated there in 1960, technology-based businesses were just starting to move in, while the National Aeronautics and Space Administration (NASA) and the U.S. Navy already had a presence there.

Young Steve loved learning about how machines worked. Paul Jobs sometimes rebuilt cars in his free time and then sold them, saving the money for Steve's college

Mountain View, California, the childhood home of Steve Jobs, is located south of San Francisco. Jobs was greatly influenced by the engineers he met there as he grew up.

education. In an oral history interview with Daniel Morrow of the Smithsonian Institution, Jobs described his father as "a genius with his hands." Paul took Steve along on trips to buy automobile parts, and Steve watched him as he fixed up the cars. Paul divided his own workbench so that his son could tinker with machines himself. They would take things apart, look at the insides, and put them back together. Though his father did not know much about electronics, what he did know he showed Steve.

Many of the neighbors were electrical engineers. Steve loved talking to them about their work. One neighbor, Larry Lang, taught him a lot about electronics. Lang bought mail-order electronics kits that could be assembled into useful products, such as radios. From watching Lang build practical electronics, Steve said he not only learned about how things work, he also came to believe that he could build anything if he put his mind to it. "These things were not mysteries anymore… They were the results of human creation, not these magical things that just appeared in one's environment," he said in the Smithsonian interview.

Lang later encouraged Steve to join a group called the Explorers Club. Hewlett-Packard, a nearby company, sponsored the club for young people who were interested in electronics. The organizers arranged field trips to places where the children could see computers, which were then gigantic. These experiences made a great impression on Steve. He wanted to learn more about computers and how to make his own.

STRUGGLING AT SCHOOL

Steve was learning a lot at home and around his neighborhood, but school was a different story. Contrary to his birth mother's dream, he was not enthusiastic about school. He was bright; his mother had taught him to read before he even began school. But though he loved reading,

Debra Lynn

Stephen Jobs

Carla

Jobs's senior yearbook photo is shown here. He graduated from Homestead High School in 1972. By then, he had found others with a similar interest in electronics and computers.

he was not interested in traditional classes. As he got a bit older, he focused his efforts on playing jokes on his teachers and classmates.

In fourth grade, Steve met a teacher who had a great impact on him. Mrs. Hill knew young Steve was a troublemaker—but a *smart* troublemaker. She understood that she had to challenge him, but that she would need to offer a tempting reward for his cooperation. What better prize for a fourth grader than candy and money? Mrs. Hill offered Steve $5 and a large lollipop if he took home a thick math workbook and finished all the problems in it. At first he thought she was crazy, but he was unable to resist. He accepted the offer and completed all of the work.

Mrs. Hill continued to challenge him in other ways, such as giving him a make-your-own-camera kit. "I think I probably learned more academically that one year than I learned in my life," he told the Smithsonian. He credited Hill and a few other teachers for setting him on the right path. Without them, he continued, "I'm sure I would have been in jail." To this day, Jobs is passionate about improving school systems so that students who are unmotivated like he was can succeed—and so that teachers like Mrs. Hill are rewarded for caring.

Steve had intelligence and abundant energy. He just needed to learn how to harness both. He was so bright that he skipped fifth grade and went right to sixth grade. He could have gone straight to high school, but his parents thought that might lead to trouble. Steve found plenty of trouble in junior high, though, and this time the problem was not his fault. Other students had such severe behavior problems that he no longer wanted to attend his school. He refused to go. His parents could not afford to send their son to a private school, so they decided to move again within Santa Clara Valley.

ENTER WOZ

In 1968, Steve began to attend Homestead High School in Cupertino, California. Many Silicon Valley engineers sent their children to this school. He found that other students at Homestead were as interested in electronics as he was. He had already made a good friend in junior high named Bill Fernandez. Steve and Bill had similar hobbies and worked on projects in Bill's garage. Bill had another friend with whom he worked on electronics. His friend was Stephen Wozniak. "Woz," as his friends called him, was five years older than Steve. Steve was impressed: Woz was the first person he had met who knew more about electronics than he did!

Steve and Woz work in the garage of the Jobs family. The two young men shared a passion for computers that would translate into a successful business partnership.

Woz and Bill showed Steve a project that they had worked on together. Woz was fascinated by computers and had wanted to build one that he could use at home. At that time, almost no one had computers in their homes. They were huge, expensive machines that were mainly used by the government and big companies. However, Woz knew that the development of silicon chips meant that computers could be made smaller. He studied computer manuals and learned how to design circuit boards, the "brains" of a computer. With spare parts from a local company, Woz and Bill worked late into the night, drinking cream soda to stay awake and energetic. They called their creation the "Cream Soda Computer." It looked nothing like today's computers— but it was a *real* computer. It had lights and switches, and no monitor or keyboard. They could give it commands using a card with holes punched into it. The computer could "read" the holes as commands and answer simple math problems by beeping.

A computer this small was news, and a local newspaper soon wanted to feature it in a story. However, when the reporter came to see the machine at work, a power glitch rendered the computer useless. Still, the Cream Soda Computer proved that Woz had great talent with the technical side of building a computer. Steve's admiration for Woz deepened.

Meanwhile, Steve had a growing talent for business. To complete a class project, he needed special electronics equipment. He decided to ask Hewlett-Packard to donate it. Rather than contact a secretary, he called the president of the company himself. William Hewlett was so struck by the young man's courage that he gave him the parts and a summer job on the company's assembly line.

Steve's other part-time job was at an electronics store called Haltek. He became knowledgeable about various components of electronics and how much they cost. Sometimes, like his dad, he would buy a broken part or machine, fix it himself, and resell it for a profit. He began to scheme: with Woz's brains and Steve's knowledge of parts, they could make some money. The two Steves were about to go into business together.

CHAPTER 2

The Two Steves

The two Steves—Jobs and Wozniak—were very different. Wozniak was laid-back and loved to joke around. He would build a computer or solve a design problem just to see if he could do it. Jobs was more ambitious, dreaming about how the computer could impact the world and how a profit could be made. It was not that Jobs was greedy—he often sold some of his rebuilt computer parts for less money to people with limited funds. But he had a head for business, while Wozniak had the technical skills. They balanced each other and got along well.

THE BLUE BOX ADVENTURE

Their first business venture was successful—but less than legal. In the early 1970s, people did not have cell phones to contact each other, so they relied on home telephones. Long-distance calls on these landlines were

Jobs and Wozniak experimented with phone phreaking—manipulating a telephone network. This is a version of a "blue box," a device they used to make free long-distance calls.

expensive. However, some people had discovered that certain sounds transmitted through the phones "tricked" the telephone companies' computers into registering a dialed number as local rather than long-distance. These tones could enable people to call any number around the world for free. The devices that transmitted these sounds were called blue boxes. Many students tried to make them. The directions were even printed in a popular magazine.

Wozniak made a blue box with an improved design. Jobs, with his work at the electronics store, saw an opportunity. He could buy the parts needed to make the box at a low cost, and Wozniak could put them together. Jobs would find customers to buy the blue box for three times the cost (less for college students) and then split the money with Wozniak. At first, they were quite successful, selling about $30,000 worth of blue boxes, but an incident made them rethink their business.

One night, Jobs and Wozniak stopped at a pizza restaurant and struck up a conversation with some men eating next to them. After a while, Jobs showed them a blue box he had with him. The men were interested in getting one, but they did not have the money. A bit later, Jobs and Wozniak left and one of the men followed. He pointed a gun at them, demanding the box. Jobs and Wozniak gave it to him. Another one of the men, whose name was Charles, explained that he wanted to pay them eventually. He even gave them his phone number before he left. However, when Jobs and Wozniak called the Chicago-area number, they were given another number for a pay phone. Charles answered the phone. He told them that he had not figured out how to make the box work. Wozniak considered tricking him into calling the police. However, it was apparent Charles was not going to pay them and that he had dangerous friends, so they hung up instead. The blue box business ended soon after that. In the documentary film *Silicon Valley: A 100 Year Renaissance*, Jobs said that Apple would never have existed without the blue box enterprise.

COLLEGE

Around that time, Jobs had his sights set on another venture: college. After visiting a friend in Oregon, he chose a small, expensive school in Portland called Reed College. His working-class parents worried about the cost, but they had made a promise to Jobs's birth mother and agreed. Once he got there, the unfocused student of his younger years came back. He found he was not interested in his classes—and his grades reflected it. Jobs later admitted that he had no idea what he

Reed College in Oregon has a reputation as a challenging school for the arts and sciences. Today, the college proudly calls Jobs a "Reedie," despite the fact that he didn't graduate.

wanted to do with his life and no idea how college was going to help him figure it out. He knew how hard his parents worked for their money, including the money paying for his education. So, after just six months, he decided to drop out of school. He was not completely disinterested in learning. He just wanted to take the classes he enjoyed. He stayed at Reed for a time, attending lectures but not earning credit or completing assignments.

Years later, in a commencement speech at Stanford University, Jobs described one of his favorite classes,

Jobs's professor at Reed College, Robert Palladino, instructs students in a calligraphy class. Jobs carried his passion for calligraphy and art into his work at Apple.

calligraphy: "I learned about serif and sans serif type-faces, about varying the amount of space between different letter combinations, about what makes great typography great." He found the art fascinating but never imagined that he would actually use this knowledge. (As the Apple Macintosh computer was being developed, Jobs insisted that multiple typefaces be included—a first for any computer.)

However, attending college as a dropout was not easy. Jobs had to sleep on the floor in friends' bedrooms. He collected soda bottles for the 5-cent deposits and used this money to buy food.

FINDING JOBS

Eventually Jobs returned home on the lookout for a new kind of life. Though the 1960s were over, Jobs was attracted to the hippie lifestyle of that time. He grew his hair and beard long. He walked around in bare feet. He became a vegetarian, for a time only eating fruit and nuts. Jobs also experimented with various drugs. He often visited a commune called All-One Farm, sharing his possessions with the community and working on the farmland. His study of Eastern religions spurred a decision to travel to India to meet some of the famous gurus that he had read about. To earn money for the trip, Jobs answered a newspaper advertisement for a job with a two-year-old video game company called Atari.

Two people play the game *Pong*, created by the video game company Atari, where Jobs worked after leaving college in 1974. Atari's games and game systems were popular into the 1980s.

Atari was the creator of the world's first video game system. Simple by today's standards, it was a sensation when it was released in 1972. The first Atari game was *Pong*, a Ping-Pong match displayed in black and white. It was so popular that the company was scrambling to keep up with the demand. At the same time, Atari wanted to create more games. Although only eighteen years old and without a degree, Jobs was hired as a design engineer. He improved games by adding elements such as sound.

He encountered some problems at his new job. He was quick to tell others that he saw flaws in their work. He could be unkind with his comments and was scheduled to work at night alone. However, he was highly valued at Atari because he had an eye for design and clever ideas about how to develop the products. Sometimes Wozniak visited Jobs, playing the Atari system while helping his friend figure out the technical configurations of a project. Wozniak helped design a game called *Breakout* for which Jobs received a large bonus. (Wozniak said the experience designing that game helped him in later designing a computer called the Apple II.)

When Jobs had saved up enough money, he and his friend Dan Kottke traveled to India and saw the great poverty of the nation. His time there made him reflect on his search for a direction in his life. He came home to California ready to work.

A HOME-BREWED COMPUTER

Jobs's position at Atari was waiting for him when he returned. He also began attending meetings of a group called the Homebrew Club with Wozniak, who was then working for Hewlett-Packard. This club of electronics and engineering fans could not stop talking about a computer kit on the market. It was called the Altair

Origin of the Name "Apple"

There are many stories about how Apple Computer got its name. One says that Jobs believed the apple was the perfect fruit and therefore a great name for the perfect computer. Yet another tale suggests that the name comes from the company Apple Records, which released albums by the Beatles, a favorite band of Jobs. The real reason, according to biographer Walter Isaacson, is that Jobs simply had apples on his mind after tending to the orchard at the All-One Farm. (He was also on an all-fruit diet at the time.) "Apple Computer" sounded like a fun, natural venture—not a cold, technological business. The name would not scare off people who were unfamiliar with technology. Wozniak liked the idea; it was simple. "Apple" just seemed right.

However, several years later, Apple Records' parent company sued Apple because of its name. Apple Computer had to promise not to get involved in the music business. As Apple introduced iTunes and other music-related products years later, it was sued again. Finally, the two companies reached a settlement in 2007, possibly putting the argument over the name to rest for good.

8800 (named partly for its 8800 microprocessor). Hobbyists could buy the kit and assemble it themselves, and much like Wozniak's Cream Soda Computer, it had lights and switches for input and output. Wozniak believed he could build another small computer that would be easier to use: he could add a keyboard to input commands and a monitor similar to that of a television to read data on the screen. (Most computers of the time were attached to a device called a Teletype.)

The development of the silicon chip had proven that a single integrated circuit could handle a number of complex functions at high speeds and storage capacity. The Altair used an improved integrated circuit called a microprocessor, making it into a central processing unit (CPU) coordinating all the functions of the computer. While the early microprocessor was not fast by today's standards, it was good enough to design a small computer around. Wozniak chose an inexpensive model for his computer and added more chips for memory. His completed design was the object of admiration by those in the Homebrew Club. He willingly shared his plans.

Jobs saw this computer as another possible joint venture, a legal moneymaking business. He convinced Wozniak to start a company with him selling circuit boards so that people could make their own computers.

Wozniak and Jobs examine a circuit board in the early days of Apple. A successful company grew out of their first order, assembled in Jobs's garage.

In a 1983 article in *TIME* magazine, Wozniak said, "Jobs didn't do one circuit, design, or piece of code... But it never crossed my mind to sell computers." The two decided to call their company Apple Computer. To raise money, Jobs sold his van and Wozniak sold two calculators. At the time, they both believed they could keep their jobs as well. A third founder, an older man named Ron Wayne, invested money, too. One of the members of the Homebrew Club owned a computer store called the Byte Shop. After a persuasive sales pitch from Jobs, the storeowner ordered fifty computers.

Jobs bought parts for $15,000 on credit, money that would need to be repaid. He asked his sister Patti and a couple of other friends to help out. Their assembly line was in the Jobs family garage. The team worked furiously and finished on time. However, there was a misunderstanding—the Byte Shop had wanted fifty assembled computers, not just circuit boards. Although the store accepted the order, Wayne bought out his share of the company for a few hundred dollars, deciding it was too risky. Jobs and Woz were not deterred, though. Apple was in business.

CHAPTER 3

Growing Apple

Jobs calculated a price for the company's first product, the Apple I: he doubled the cost of the materials and added a 33 percent markup—for a total of $666.66. While the company continued to sell this model, Wozniak looked for ways to improve it.

The Apple I did not look much like a computer as we know it. It had no keyboard, no monitor to display graphics, and no case. People had to buy these parts separately. The people who bought the computers from the Byte Shop received cases from a local woodworking shop, so their Apple Is looked like typewriters in wooden cases. This might not sound like much, but the Apple I was much easier to use than the computers assembled from kits. Programs were loaded onto the computer using cassette tapes. They had to be input each time the user turned on the computer, but it was easier than typing thousands of lines of commands in programming language. Woz built the Apple I to run an early programming language called BASIC, so people could play games on it.

FROM I TO II

While working to build the Apple I, Wozniak had ideas for the next Apple computer. Jobs did, too. Even though the Apple I was easier to assemble and operate than the other computers of that time, the average person with no knowledge of electronics had little interest in it. The Apple I was a gaming and hobbyist computer; it would not make people's lives easier. Jobs wanted the next computer,

This wooden case houses an Apple I computer, the first Apple product, which debuted in 1976. The keyboard and video monitor were purchased separately.

the Apple II, to be in every home and school. To achieve this, it would have to be the complete package—both entertaining and useful. Wozniak went to work. In 1977, the Apple II was finished. It displayed in color, had sound, and came with its own case. It allowed for a printer to be hooked up to it—and even controls for games. Its eight expansion slots allowed for additional memory, processor accelerators, and video cards. But the great allure of the Apple II was the software it was able to run. Spreadsheet and word processing programs interested both schools and businesses.

Apple needed more parts to fulfill additional orders, so an influx of money was essential to buy the parts. Apple needed investors who believed that they would get their money back and more; these investors had to trust that Apple Computer had a future.

While Jobs had great powers of persuasion, he was still young. Some older investors looked at the longhaired business owner in jeans and were not convinced of Apple's longevity. Luckily, after being turned down by one investor, Jobs found Mark Markkula. Markkula was a young investor who had worked for the company Intel. He had made his fortune in Intel stock, and he believed in the future of computers. After talking to Jobs, he believed in Apple. Markkula supplied money to expand the company and used his reputation to gain more capital. He took on a management role as an employee and even wrote programs.

THE APPLE II

The Apple II (or Apple][, as it appeared on its nameplate) was unveiled to the public in April 1977 at the West Coast Computer Faire. Wozniak had streamlined the components as much as he could, eliminating unnecessary chips. Meanwhile, Jobs's eye for design had shaped the case, a unique feature in the personal computer market. He made sure the cables and extra accessories were hidden so that it looked like anyone could operate the machine. An Apple II owner only needed to connect the computer to his or her television and plug it into the wall. It was not the cheapest personal computer on the market—it cost $1,298 with just 4 kilobytes (kB) of memory—but it had excellent color graphics. Two Apple programmers, who were high school students, wrote programs to show off its sound and color. Also, unlike other less expensive computers of the time, the Apple II was built to easily add multiple devices, such as game paddles and storage units. Plus, it looked like a computer, not a hastily crafted project.

Apple's logo changed just in time for the unveiling of the Apple II. The company's first logo was an old-fashioned picture of Isaac Newton sitting under an apple tree. The new one was a single apple with a bite missing. It was filled with stripes of color, a reminder of the Apple II's color display. Apple was the talk of the trade show.

The Apple II Plus, released in 1979, sold for $1,195, less than the original Apple II. It came with more memory, too. Apple employees constantly looked for ways to improve their products.

Jobs worked to market the Apple II to the average person and to schools. In this way, Apple was different from other companies. Most companies sold to businesses, government agencies, and people who worked with computers as a hobby. Jobs thought Apple could change the market by making computers accessible to everyone.

In fact, many people at Apple had that feeling. Bill Fernandez, school friend of Jobs and Wozniak, was an employee of the company at this time. David A. Price's book *The Pixar Touch* relates how Fernandez remembered the work environment: "There was, at least for me, a tangible feeling of magic in the air." He and others felt they were giving "power to the people," or putting the power of computing into everyone's hands.

In a 1996 piece for *Newsweek*, Wozniak agreed that building Apple had little to do with "greed or ego." Instead, the enterprise was focused on giving the average person access to the same technology as the most powerful institutions. Apple was a company for everyday people, run by ordinary people. As if to reflect this, Jobs and Wozniak dressed in jeans and allowed their employees to dress casually as well.

Orders for the Apple II started to fly in. As when the Apple I was in production, the company had its eye on improving the product. The idea for a new storage device originated when Mark Markkula was loading a program he had written onto his Apple II. It took over two minutes. Markkula asked Wozniak to figure out how to create a better storage system. At that time, people could use a cassette recorder to store and retrieve programs and data, but it was unreliable, slow, and inefficient. The device basically worked much like audiocassette tapes: the user needed to know exactly where a program was on the tape.

Markkula asked Wozniak to consider a floppy disk drive for the Apple II. These disk drives read and record data on small, circular bendable pieces of plastic called floppy disks. Wozniak took on the challenge of designing a disk drive for the Apple II. The Disk II floppy drive had a positive reception from the public and computer engineers. First available in July 1978, it was also the least expensive on the market and could store more data than many other drives at that time.

Apple did not write much software for its computers. However, when software companies saw what the Apple II could do, they began writing software specifically for it. Some of this software could be used in business, such as the VisiCalc spreadsheet program. Short for "visible calculations," VisiCalc allowed users to input numbers for quick calculations. This time-saving device was so popular that many businesses wanted to buy the Apple II just to run it.

Another version of the Apple II was released in 1979. It came with much more memory—16 kB of random access memory (RAM), rather than 4 kB—and was called the Apple II Plus. Also offered was Apple's first printer, the SilenType, with the word processing program Apple Writer. Though the printer and program had their problems, they made people excited about a future without typewriters. Apple was headed in the right direction.

APPLE'S IPO

By 1980, Apple Computer had grown. It had about one thousand employees, a far cry from the few people in Jobs's garage just a few years earlier. However, it needed still more employees and capital to grow. Many companies start as private companies, getting start-up money from a handful of individuals and venture capital firms, just as Apple got money from Jobs, Wozniak, Wayne, and Markkula. Those early investors take a risk and hope that the company will be successful so that they can get their money back—and more. When a private company reaches a certain size and point in its production, it may become public. This means people in the public can invest in the company by buying stock. Going public gives the initial owners the chance to reap some money for their hard work. Cash flows into the company through its initial public offering, or IPO, of shares.

On December 12, 1980, Apple Computer became a public company. Shares of Apple began the day selling at $22 each. Over 4.5 million shares sold out in just minutes. This was the largest IPO since the Ford Motor Company went public in 1956. By the end of the day, shares were worth $29 each, and the company was worth $1.778 billion. At least forty Apple employees became instant millionaires through their shares.

GROWING THE APPLE MARKET

"One of the things that built Apple IIs was schools buying Apple IIs," asserted Jobs in his interview with Daniel Morrow of the Smithsonian. Apple IIs were selling well to schools, topping any other company's computers. Apple computers were introducing a generation to computers that otherwise would not have been exposed to them until much later in life. Jobs believed that Apple's products had the potential to become even more popular in the school market.

In the Smithsonian interview, Jobs estimated that about 10 percent of schools had a computer in 1979. Realizing how much paperwork and decision-making went into a school buying a computer, Jobs and some others at Apple decided they wanted to give an Apple computer to every elementary and high school in America. That was about one hundred thousand computers. While this was a significant investment for Apple, a certain federal law allowed companies to donate scientific tools to universities in exchange for a tax break. Jobs figured they would not lose as much financially if Apple could get this tax break. Besides the company being seen as charitable, the schools might invest in additional Apple products. The students working with Apple computers might even ask their parents to buy them for their homes. All Apple had to do was persuade Congress to change the tax-break law to cover the donation of computers to elementary and high schools.

Over the course of about two weeks in 1982, Jobs met and talked with about two-thirds of the members of the U.S. House of Representatives and over half of the U.S. Senate. When it came time for a vote on the bill, it passed in the House with an overwhelming majority. However, it was not even brought to a vote in the Senate due to quarrels between the political parties.

Though the federal action died, some lawmakers in California were interested. They passed a state law allowing Apple state tax breaks if computers were donated to public schools. Ten thousand California schools received computers through Apple's Kids Can't Wait program. Apple persuaded software companies to donate software as well.

THE APPLE III

Though the VisiCalc spreadsheet program had helped Apple gain entry into the business market, it was still way behind other companies in this area. At that time, IBM was the most trusted maker of business computers. Apple decided to go head-to-head with IBM in engineering the Apple III.

The Apple III sounded great on paper. It was the first Apple with a built-in floppy disk drive. Unveiled in May 1980, it had twice the memory of the Apple II and ran twice as fast. As head of design for the project, Jobs had wanted a small, good-looking machine. He specified sizes to his engineers. He also asked that no fan be built into the computer to further reduce its size and noise. The lack of a cooling system in combination with a protective metal bottom added up to trouble. As the Apple III was running, it would heat up to such a degree that the chips popped out of place. As a troubleshooting technique, people dropped the Apple IIIs to jam the chips back into position.

Steve Wozniak, Then and Now

Steve Wozniak was born August 11, 1950, in San Jose, California. He was the son of an engineer and became interested in electronics at an early age. He went to college at several schools, including the University of California at Berkeley. Wozniak left college after his third year for lack of money, and he began working for Hewlett-Packard, designing calculators. He then left to found Apple with his friend Steve Jobs. (He later returned to Berkeley and finished his degree.)

Wozniak worked hard to make Apple computers easy to use for nonengineers. This was an important step in putting a computer in every home, something almost unimaginable at that time. Though Wozniak would leave Apple as a designer in 1985, he says on his Web site Woz.org (http://www.woz.org): "I never left. I keep a tiny residual salary to this day because that's where my loyalty should be forever."

Though rumors fly about quarreling between the two Steves, Wozniak denies them, stating that they never argued. Wozniak acknowledges that Jobs was a good friend to him and that it took the two of them to make Apple take off. On Woz.org, he says: "I could not do what [Jobs did]: I'm a techie who likes to do techie things all the time and there's not time left over to stay up on the latest technologies and the big picture." Upon hearing of Jobs's resignation as CEO in 2011, Wozniak praised Jobs on Bloomberg Television's *Bloomberg West*, calling him "the greatest technology business leader of our time."

Today, Wozniak is passionate about charity work and has provided computers, laptops, and technical support to many schools. He even teaches classes on how to use technology. He is also very active in communicating with people on his Web site; anyone can write and ask him a question. He spends hours answering as many as he can and posts the replies for his readers to see. His humor and intelligence are woven into every answer. Reflecting Wozniak's ideals, the Web site proclaims that it is a "free exchange of information, the way it always should be."

Wendell Sander, chief designer of the Apple III, believed the main problem with the computer was that the product was rushed out the door. Though many blamed Jobs for his uncompromising style demands, Sander did not. Other employees agreed, saying that everyone had great ideas to contribute to the machine; the problem was that everyone's ideas were used. They had implemented too many improvements at once.

An estimated fourteen thousand Apple IIIs had to be replaced. Two more models were released as attempts

Despite attempts to fix the Apple III's problems with improved models, people distrusted it. The Apple III Plus was on the market for just four months before the company pulled the plug on all models.

to fix the problems: a revised Apple III and the Apple III Plus. Finally, Apple discontinued the Apple III in April 1984, just shy of four years after its introduction. The failure of the Apple III was the company's first major setback and a costly mistake.

SHAKE-UPS AT APPLE

While the Apple III was struggling in the marketplace, the mood changed at Apple headquarters. Tensions increased among some employees. One cause was the treatment of some workers prior to Apple's IPO. Under Jobs's advisement, not all employees had been given the stock options that made Jobs, Wozniak, and others rich. Even Dan Kottke, a friend and one of the first Apple employees, was left out. (Wozniak sold some of his shares to these people to make amends.)

After the stock took off, Jobs and Wozniak had the wealth to acquire whatever they wanted. Jobs bought a mansion, a sports car, and a motorcycle. However, he was still the man who had traveled to India looking for the meaning of life, and he struggled with owning these material possessions. People who visited his house were surprised to see there was almost nothing in it. Jobs also donated to charities, including one to fight blindness and smallpox around the world.

Steve Wozniak and a group of California middle-school students dance while holding Apple PowerBook laptop computers. Wozniak frequently donated computers and taught technology classes for children.

But all was not at peace in his personal life. Jobs's girlfriend had given birth to a baby girl, Lisa, in 1978. Jobs vehemently denied that he was the baby's father for two years. In 1980, after a paternity test, he finally accepted responsibility and agreed to provide financially for young Lisa.

Wozniak made some major purchases, too, including an airplane that he learned to fly himself. Unfortunately, on February 7, 1981, Wozniak crashed his plane. He and his fiancée were seriously injured. After he recovered, Wozniak took time off from the company. This was not wholly unexpected, as Wozniak had disagreed with many of the decisions surrounding the Apple III. He needed a break from the business. He married and went back to college. Wozniak would return to Apple again in 1983, but just for a couple of years. He retired in 1985 to spend more time with his family, the same year that he and Jobs received the National Technology Award from President Ronald Reagan.

CHAPTER 4

A Changing Apple

Apple Computer had exploded after its public offering. Its success put Steve Jobs in the public eye. *TIME* magazine nearly named him Man of the Year for 1982 but eventually substituted "The Computer." It was Apple's computers that had taken the nation by storm and inspired people to adopt computer technology. As Apple's chairman of the board, Jobs was at the top of his profession.

Apple learned that IBM was preparing a personal computer to rival the Apple II, which continued to sell briskly after the release of the Apple III. Apple would need a new product to counter IBM's. As part of a 1979 agreement with Xerox, Jobs asked to tour the company's Palo Alto Research Center (PARC). What he discovered there was the future. Xerox's engineers had invented a graphical user interface (GUI). With the GUI, users could use an object called a mouse to interact with the computer, rather than type commands.

In his interview with Daniel Morrow of the Smithsonian, Jobs remembered, "Within ten minutes of seeing the graphical user interface stuff, just knowing that every computer would work this way some day; it was so obvious once you saw it." Xerox's GUI was not without its trouble spots, but there were windows and menu options, enough to inspire Jobs.

THE LISA

Jobs envisioned that Apple's graphical user interface computer would truly change the market. He hand-picked engineers to build the machine, which was given the code name "Lisa." In Owen Linzmayer's book *Apple Confidential 2.0*, Trip Hawkins, one of the team, remembered Jobs "had an incredible ability to rally people towards some common cause." In the Lisa computer, Jobs believed he had more than a cause. According to Hawkins, Jobs often told his team, "We'll make it so important that it will make a dent in the universe."

The Lisa's GUI featured icons on which the user could click to begin applications such as word processing and drawing programs. An abundance of hardware added up to a hefty forty-eight pounds (twenty-two kilograms). However, the Lisa looked stylish, the signature of Jobs's involvement. Jobs boldly predicted a sale of fifty thousand computers in its first year. The Lisa appeared on the market in January 1983.

Unfortunately, Lisa's hardware was so expensive that the computer was priced at $9,995, a cost out of reach for most home computer users. For businesses, while the computer was packed with programs, it ran too slow. (The

Apple designed the Lisa for the business market. Notice the software on the screen and the rectangular mouse.

Lisa inspired a knock-knock joke: "Knock knock." "Who's there?" *Wait 20 seconds.* "Lisa.") The result was that the Lisa and the improved Lisa 2 were only offered for two years before they were discontinued.

The Apple board had asked Jobs to step down from the Lisa project in 1980, but his management was still blamed for the failure. Jobs felt great pressure to follow up the Apple II with an equally successful product. Technology was changing quickly in the marketplace, and he feared that if Apple did not make good use of the GUI technology, competitors might soon eclipse the company.

JOBS EYES THE MACINTOSH

The project that would save Apple was already in development, headed by engineer Jef Raskin. True to Apple's mission, Raskin envisioned a computer for the average person. He called the computer the Macintosh after a kind of apple. Raskin persuaded Apple's board to allow him to begin work on the Macintosh in September 1979. Jobs was an early critic of the product, but this did not deter Raskin. He maintained his goal to keep the computer user-friendly and affordable.

After Jobs was asked to leave the Lisa team, he became interested in Raskin's Macintosh. Because of Jobs's initial reaction to the Macintosh, Raskin resisted working with him, and at first he did not have to. Jobs became involved

Hundreds of Macintosh computers sit on a manufacturing line during a testing period in Freemont, California, in March 1984.

in developing the Macintosh's hardware while Raskin concentrated on software. It was Jobs who insisted the Macintosh have a mouse. Raskin asked that the mouse have only one button so that it would be easy for new users.

After Jobs moved to take over software development, Raskin resigned in March 1982. He had lost control over his personal project and no longer wanted to put up with Jobs's demands. (In 1987, when the one millionth Macintosh was produced, it was given to Raskin.)

After IBM's successful introduction of its PC (personal computer), Apple tried to get the Macintosh on the market quickly. Jobs asked his team to work harder and longer hours, as many as ninety hours a week. He invited the best engineers from other divisions, such as the Apple II division, to join his group. He encouraged them to be proud of the "Mac."

In the PBS documentary *Triumph of the Nerds*, designer Andy Hertzfeld remembered Jobs's overwhelming enthusiasm. Hertzfeld had been a member of the Apple II team when Jobs approached his cubicle and announced he was needed for the Mac project. Though Hertzfeld requested to work a few more days on the Apple II to finish his programming, Jobs insisted, "You gotta start now." He meant immediately. Hertzfeld watched as Jobs unplugged his computer, erasing the code that he was working on. He followed helplessly as Jobs drove his machine to a new office and placed it on a desk. "Well, you're working on the Mac now," Jobs said.

With the plucking of talent from other divisions, rivalries and jealousies began to creep into Apple. Jobs praised his Mac team members as "artists." He had them sign the inside casing of the Mac, just as painters signed their works of art. Meanwhile, the Macintosh team was feeling the pressure of being Jobs's chosen few. Some remember Jobs making them feel worthless one minute and then on top of the world the next. Other Apple executives were watching Jobs's management and wondered if this kind of motivation would really work.

By 1984, Jobs's management practices began to strain his relationships with other Apple employees. As he pushed to make the Macintosh the next big success, tempers flared.

SCULLEY TAKES THE HELM

When Jobs was not working on the Macintosh project, he was looking for a new president for Apple. He searched for someone who would know how to market products, and he set his sights on the young president of Pepsi-Cola USA, John Sculley. At Pepsi, Sculley had success in challenging archrival Coca-Cola in the marketplace. Who better to help Apple challenge IBM?

As Sculley relates in *Triumph of the Nerds*, Jobs aggressively pursued him and asked him a now-famous question: "Do you want to sell sugar water for the rest of your life, or do you want to come with me and change the world?" Sculley thought he would spend the rest of his life wondering about the opportunity if he didn't seize it. He was named president and CEO of Apple in April 1983.

Under Sculley's supervision, a commercial was produced to introduce the Macintosh to the world during the 1984 Super Bowl. The commercial would become one of the most famous of all time. In it, a woman wearing a Macintosh shirt confronts a dark image representing the cold, impersonal business world of IBM. She shatters the image, a metaphor for the Mac bringing fresh, bright ideas into the personal computing world.

ENTER THE MAC

Jobs officially introduced the Macintosh computer on January 24, 1984, at an Apple shareholders' meeting, calling it "insanely great." Then he let the Macintosh introduce itself. A voice from the computer told the audience to "never trust a computer you can't lift" and described Jobs as "the man who's been like a father to me." This was the sort of showmanship at which Jobs excelled. The crowd leapt to its feet, applauding the "talking" computer. Jobs showed its graphics and the multitude of programs it included, such as MacPaint, MacWrite, and a chess game. Its many applications did not compromise its speed.

Jobs boldly predicted Apple would sell a half million Macintoshes in a year. The low cost of such importance to Raskin had not been possible. The final price tag was $2,495. Nevertheless, the computers sold briskly at first. However, some criticisms began to emerge: it had too little memory, the monitor was small and only black-and-white, and it had no number or function keys. The sales slowed to a trickle.

Yes, the IBM PC was harder to use, but it was less expensive and could do more. The slump of the Macintosh hit Apple hard. In 1985, about one-fifth of the company's employees were laid off, accompanying its first-ever quarterly loss. Two targets of blame were Jobs and Sculley.

The Macintosh and Desktop Publishing

Before Jobs exited Apple, he backed a deal that would eventually make the Macintosh a great success in one area of the business world: publishing. Jobs believed in the "killer app," an application that is so useful that a consumer wants to buy the computer just to use it. He found that application in a programming language provided by the company Adobe. Adobe PostScript was a page description language that worked in conjunction with an "interpreter" in a computer printer. The language positioned lines, shapes, and other graphical elements, as well as placed and formatted text. A PostScript interpreter was built into the Apple LaserWriter printer introduced in 1985. The PageMaker software program, created by the company Aldus and later acquired by Adobe, was also offered with the Macintosh. PageMaker was layout software that allowed users to "lay out" a page and print out the image exactly as it appeared on the screen. This kind of software is called WYSIWYG software, with WYSIWYG standing for "what you see is what you get."

The combination of PageMaker, PostScript, and the LaserWriter was the start of desktop publishing, which is designing combinations of text and graphics on a computer and then printing them as they appear. For the first time, anyone with these products had a platform from which to produce documents, such as brochures and newsletters, which looked like they came from a professional publishing house. For a while, Page-Maker and PostScript were only available for Macintoshes and were a tremendous boost for the product.

Jobs made a plea to the board of directors. He said that Sculley, as Apple's president and CEO, had steered the company wrong. But the board disagreed. They pointed to Jobs's hands-on involvement in two projects: the Lisa and the Macintosh. Both appeared to be failures, and Jobs's management of his teams had led to a hostile work environment. Although he was allowed to keep his title of chairman, Jobs knew that it was in name only. He was asked to move out of his office and across the street, which seemed to him a kind of banishment. Although he requested to work on products, no one accepted his offers. Jobs knew that he no longer had a place at Apple. At thirty years old, Steve Jobs resigned in September 1985 from the company he had founded.

Jobs's departure from Apple caused mixed emotions. Apple employee Larry Tesler addressed the complex reactions in *Triumph of the Nerds*: "Everyone had been terrorized by Steve Jobs at some point or another, and so there was a certain relief... But on the other hand, I think there was an incredible respect for Steve Jobs by the very same people."

Another employee from that time, Bill Atkinson, agreed: "Steve really did make the product better without even knowing exactly how the engineer was doing it." Tesler, Atkinson, and their coworkers were worried. What would happen to Apple Computer without its visionary founder?

CHAPTER 5

NeXT and Pixar

As much as Steve Jobs was behind the tension in the halls of Apple during the development of the Lisa and the Macintosh, his employees strongly believed in him as the visionary of the company. After Apple, Jobs needed a new vision. He found it after having coffee with Paul Berg, a renowned biochemist working at Stanford University. The two talked about the possibilities of using computers to simulate experiments and creating software to teach students about scientific research. Jobs thought an inexpensive, high-powered computer geared toward universities would fill a need in the market.

He began a new company, NeXT, with the aim of delivering this product. He asked a few of his Apple colleagues to join him. John Sculley and the board tried unsuccessfully to sue him, angry that he was taking Apple's talent with him. Jobs was amused. "It's hard to think that a $2 billion company with 4,300-plus people couldn't

Steve Jobs introduces his NeXT computer system in October 1988, three years after leaving Apple. Jobs hoped to break into the university and business computer market.

compete with six people in blue jeans," he told *Newsweek* in September 1985.

Jobs set up an expensive new office space near the Xerox PARC. He hired an interior decorator as a full-time employee and famous designer Paul Rand to create the company's logo. (Rand suggested the use of the lowercase "e" in the company's name: NeXT.) Jobs was filled with new goals and ideals. He pledged not to make the same mistakes he made at Apple, and he renewed his ambition to make affordable computers that would change the world. He resolved to listen to his potential customers' needs and wants. He continued to flex his charisma and lure the brightest employees to his side with an invitation to help him change the world.

ANOTHER VENTURE

While Jobs was trying to get one company off the ground, he also purchased another. A few months before he resigned from Apple, he had heard about a group of engineers experimenting with computer-generated imagery (CGI). At the time, they were working for George Lucas, the creator of the *Star Wars* movies. Lucas thought CGI could replace his use of models in film. So far they had used the technology very little, creating a few minutes of a movie and a short animated film.

By 1985, Lucas had found this technology division too expensive to support. Rather than disbanding them, he allowed the group to find a buyer. The team, led by Ed Catmull and Alvy Ray Smith, had developed a computer that could process images at an unbelievably fast rate. They called it the Pixar Image Computer. When Jobs examined the group's hardware and software, he thought the image-making computer could be sold to hospitals for 3-D X-rays and similar imaging, or to businesses to create commercials. Jobs made a low offer, which was turned down. Just a few months later, he submitted his offer again. By that time, Lucas was desperate to get rid of the group and accepted $5 million, with Jobs agreeing to invest $5 million more in the business. The new company, under CEO Jobs, was called Pixar.

Unlike Apple and NeXT, Pixar operated with much less direction from Jobs, partly because of distance. The group resisted Jobs's efforts to move them from San Raphael to Silicon Valley, more than two hours away. A representative traveled to NeXT headquarters each week to report on progress, something employees dreaded in their first unsuccessful years.

Although the core group of employees had their hearts set on using their technology to make movies, the team had been acquired to produce computers. However, the Pixar Image Computers were priced at $135,000 each. Few businesses could invest in one, though the U.S. government purchased some to analyze images captured on spy satellites. A lower-cost model was produced beginning in 1987. Though much less expensive—$29,500—the

Pixar Image Computer II was still too pricey and complicated for the mainstream market. Meanwhile, Catmull and Smith had an idea: a movie created with the computer might promote sales.

INVESTING IN NEXT

Back at NeXT headquarters, Jobs was losing money fast with nothing yet in production. Though he had wanted the company to be owned only by himself and his employees, by 1986 it needed outside revenue. Texas billionaire H. Ross Perot offered an investment of $20 million after seeing a TV program about Jobs and other entrepreneurs. This was more than even Jobs himself had invested. Even better for a company hoping to produce computers for universities, Stanford and Carnegie-Mellon invested money in NeXT.

By this time, the company's low-cost higher-education computer was surpassing the original price point of $1,000. Jobs fell into his old habits of stressing style over expense. The NeXT Computer, nicknamed the "Cube," had a cubical casing designed—for an unknown price—by famous industrial designer Hartmut Esslinger. Jobs insisted on the newest technology, such as trading the floppy disk drive for an optical disk drive, which he believed was the way of the future. Yet another cost was building an automated factory so that the computer could be manufactured completely on the grounds. Most computer companies had subcontractors assemble their hardware off-property, but

Texas billionaire H. Ross Perot was so confident in the abilities of Steve Jobs that he became the largest investor in NeXT.

Jobs fell in love with the idea that everything would be created in one place. He imagined people taking tours of the facility. Perot, who might have helped with the business side of the company, seemed to defer to Jobs. The NeXT factory and offices were beautiful—and expensive—but the company was late in delivering the product.

Finally, in October 1988, the NeXT Computer was unveiled. Before this moment, the inner workings of the company had been a secret; no one knew what to expect. Because of Jobs's unfailing enthusiasm for his product, people already wanted one. A NeXT employee called a newspaper to buy pages to advertise the computer's unveiling. The newspaper worker wondered why to even bother: everyone knew October 12 was the day. Jobs hired a theater director to help set up the unveiling at a music hall. The stage was set with a black backdrop behind a vase of flowers, the computer covered in a black cloth, and Steve Jobs. He talked for three hours, expressing the many ways in which the computer system was "revolutionary." Though it could not run other companies' software, he implied its own was so good that it did not matter.

Jobs demonstrated the software from afar. Many suspect it was not quite ready yet. The music software made a positive impression with the acoustics of the music hall, as did the "digital library," which included *Webster's Collegiate Dictionary*. The showmanship worked, and when Jobs announced the cost—$6,500—the audience applauded. He described the computer as "plug and play," meaning the user only needed to plug it in. The Macintosh was the only other easy-to-assemble machine like this at the time.

The computer's undeniable jewel was its operating system, NeXTSTEP. It had a multitasking graphical user interface that was intuitive to use and pleasing to the eye. (Many features, such as a dock on the desktop for applications, are still used today.) Jobs announced that IBM would license a form of the operating system (OS) for its own computers. This news seemed to seal it—the NeXT Computer System, though expensive, was the "next step" in computers.

Orders for the Cube, however, did not come in as planned. Despite the initial fanfare, it came down to cost. How much could the average college student pay? How much could a professor ask his or her school to spend? A company called Sun Microsystems was far outselling NeXT, having marketed a product it called a "workstation." Jobs also had the problem of persuading people to give up their old computers. Many people who did buy the Cube found that it was slow and limited in software.

Two years after the first NeXT computer was introduced, Jobs unveiled the high-end NeXTcube (a more powerful replacement for the original Cube) and the more affordable NeXTstation. Despite being faster and more colorful, both were still much more expensive than a Mac, and neither could run other companies' software. The Sun workstations and Apple Macs continued outselling NeXT computers.

No one except a select few knew how much trouble the company was in. Perot was one of those. He complained that the money he had invested had not been managed well, and he resigned from the board of directors in 1991. In 1992, NeXT sold just twenty thousand computers. Other companies sold that many computers in a single week. The following year, the company laid off about half the employees in an effort to cut costs. Jobs's dream of the ultimate computer—basically, a better Macintosh—had seemingly failed.

Microsoft Versus Apple

By the 1990s, the two major competitors in the PC market were Microsoft and Apple. Microsoft was a software company that had created applications for the Macintosh, such as Excel, in the early 1980s. Bill Gates, one of Microsoft's founders, had worked to create the MS-DOS operating system for IBM PC-compatible computers. This OS was not a graphical user interface. Users had to know what commands to enter in order to run programs. Gates later developed an interface that he called Windows to run on top of MS-DOS. It took several years until it was as easy to use as the GUI in the Mac. When it finally debuted, Apple thought it was so similar to the point-and-click OS in the Mac that it could be considered stolen property. Apple sued Microsoft in 1988. It was not until 1994 and many versions of Windows later that the case was decided—and Apple lost. Windows 95 replaced MS-DOS as a true GUI operating system. Microsoft software and applications flooded the market, quickly making Gates the richest man in the world.

PIXAR TASTES SUCCESS

Jobs's other company, Pixar, was losing an estimated $10 million a year. However, a Pixar-produced short film called *Tin Toy* had won an Academy Award in 1988. Appreciating the talent of the animating artists, Jobs kept them on even as he laid off many other employees. Only Jobs's personal investment was keeping Pixar afloat.

Pixar began producing commercials, specializing in giving human characteristics to inanimate objects like an orange and a bottle of mouthwash. However, the money was not enough. Jobs and Smith frequently had shouting matches at meetings. "It wasn't really working," said Smith according to David A. Price's book *The Pixar Touch*. "In fact, that's being kind of gentle. We should have failed. But it seemed to me that Steve just would not suffer defeat."

A big break came in 1990. The head of Walt Disney Studios, Jeffrey Katzenberg, had an interest in making a film using Pixar technology. The final agreement stated that Disney would have control over the film script penned by Pixar, and Pixar would make the movie using its software for 3-D modeling and animation. (The software was called Menv, short for "modeling environment.") Disney would also own the movie. Though it seemed a one-sided deal, Pixar needed a big break in Hollywood, and Disney could provide that. John Lasseter, an ex-Disney animator who had joined the Pixar team, had been the main creative force behind the *Tin Toy* movie. He became the lead writer for the script that evolved into the movie *Toy Story*.

While *Toy Story* was in production, Jobs tried to sell Pixar. He was still losing money, as Disney only covered some of the costs of production. He was close to making a deal with Microsoft in 1994 when he suddenly changed his mind. Perhaps realizing that something special was being created, he stuck with his company. In fact, he became so convinced that *Toy Story* would be a hit that he arranged for the company to go public just a week after its release. Disney's marketing resources, meanwhile, helped build excitement for the movie.

A CHANGE OF FORTUNE

While NeXT's hardware was a failure, its operating system was the opposite. Other companies wanted to license the easy-to-use GUI for their computers. Another version of the OS was developed to run on IBM-compatible computers powered by Intel chips. This popular business product finally helped NeXT record its first profit in 1994. Jobs saw a chance to salvage his company through its software.

John Lasseter, shown above with two characters from *Toy Story*, was the creative force behind Pixar's early successes in computer-animated films.

Good news came to Pixar as well. When *Toy Story* was released on November 22, 1995, it was an instant sensation. It was the rare children's film that captivated adults, too. Movie critics hailed it as one of the best movies of the year; it would later be nominated for an Academy Award for Best Picture. In its first twelve days, the movie earned $64.7 million, and it would go on to be the highest-grossing movie of the year.

The buzz from the film made Pixar's IPO an amazing success. Shares started at $22 and closed at $39, raising $139.7 million in just one day. This made Jobs and several others multimillionaires. Jobs's money troubles were over. All he needed was a relationship with a company that would guarantee his NeXT OS would continue to exist. He would soon hear that a familiar company was hoping to purchase a new operating system.

CHAPTER 6

A Warm Welcome

While Jobs was working to make NeXT a success, Apple was experiencing highs and lows of its own. The Macintosh, which had been slow in selling at first, had exploded in the marketplace. Its easy-to-use operating system had made it the computer for everyone. The computer was in homes, businesses, schools, and libraries. By March 1987, more than one million Macs had been produced. The product was a huge success. Apple rode the wave of money coming in.

In the early 1990s, the original Mac was tweaked several times so that new models could be placed on the market. However, the few brand-new Apple products, including a handheld personal digital assistant (PDA) called the Newton and the Pippin gaming system, did not last on the market. John Sculley, the CEO who had battled Jobs and seemingly won, left in 1993. Another CEO, Michael

Spindler, came and went. Apple was losing its place in a market flooded with low-cost computers. At one point, the company was losing a reported $1 billion a year. The next CEO, Gil Amelio, who took the lead in 1996, decided that a new operating system was needed. The GUI of Apple was no longer unique. Knowing they needed the new OS fast, he planned to acquire an existing one.

Family: A Good Influence

In 1989, Jobs met a graduate student named Laurene Powell when he spoke to her class at Stanford. He was so impressed by her that he cancelled a business dinner that same night so that they could eat together. In an interview with Steve Lohr of *New York Times Magazine*, he recalled, "I thought to myself, If this is my last night on Earth, would I rather spend it at a business meeting or with this woman?" They continued to date, and then in 1991, Powell discovered she was pregnant. Proving this was different from his previous relationship, Jobs agreed to marry. The two were married at Yosemite National Park with a Zen Buddhist monk officiating. A son, Reed Paul, was born that September. They later had two daughters, Erin Sienna and Eve.

Though his passion for his job never flagged, Jobs wanted a family life, too. He did not want to be a workaholic anymore. Of fatherhood, he told Lohr, "[I] just try to be as good a father to them as my father was to me." He became a bigger part of his daughter Lisa's life as well. She lived with the family for a time when she was a teenager.

Steve Jobs and Laurene Powell Jobs attend the opening of a Pixar exhibit at the Museum of Modern Art in New York. Ms. Powell Jobs cofounded a natural-foods company and is involved in many charities.

A NEW STEVE JOBS?

Jobs made a call to Amelio in November 1996. Amelio agreed to hear what Jobs had to say. Typical of Jobs, his sales presentation wowed both Amelio and the board members who were present. Jobs showed four videos at the same time on a desktop using his operating system. This was something the Mac could not do. He said NeXT-STEP, now called OpenStep, was ahead of the OS market by at least five years. He suggested that Apple would not only want OpenStep, it would also want to buy the whole company so that the system's developers could tailor the OS to Apple's needs. Jobs's spell had been cast. Amelio and Apple agreed to buy NeXT for a sale price of $400 million. In addition, Jobs was offered a management role at Apple, but he declined. One reason he gave was his dedication to his family.

Jobs seemed different from the man who had believed that he ruled Apple years before. A longtime employee at Pixar saw the change in him at that company as well. In a 1997 profile in the *New York Times Magazine*, Pamela Kerwin explained, "After the first three words out of your mouth, he'd interrupt you and say, 'OK, here's how I see things.' It isn't like that anymore. He listens a lot more, and he's more relaxed, more mature."

Jobs conceded that he trusted people more after his experiences. At Pixar, for example, he had learned

Apple computers became commonplace in schools in the 1990s. However, without an innovative new product, Apple's sales began to slip. By 1996, the company's profits were hitting an all-time low.

that the right people could get the job done well without micromanagement. He told Jeff Goodell of *Rolling Stone*, "What's important is that you have a faith in people, that they're basically good and smart, and if you give them tools, they'll do wonderful things with them." Rather than insisting that he be involved in every part of a project, he realized that he did not need to be.

BACK ON TOP

In an interview with the Smithsonian before his return to Apple, Jobs had lamented the state of the company, blaming the situation on John Sculley. He maintained that Apple had been founded as a company with the goal of making excellent computers for everyone, but it had turned into a company that cared only about profits. Jobs had wanted the Mac to be an "appliance," indispensable to a household, much like a refrigerator or a stove. Now he was back with Apple in the role of adviser. He was "the face" to inspire the company.

As CEO, Gil Amelio had been making decisions to try to change the financial state of the company since 1996, but Apple was still losing money. Things were not turning around fast enough. By July 1997, the board of directors asked Amelio to step down. They offered the position to Jobs. He declined the permanent position but agreed to be the interim CEO as well as a member of the board until the right person was hired. He even refused a salary, except for $1 a year so that he could be on the company's health care plan.

One of the first deals that Jobs arranged was with an unlikely ally—Bill Gates of Microsoft. Gates's company offered an investment of $150 million in Apple in exchange for some changes favorable to Microsoft. Jobs made the announcement at the 1997 Macworld Expo. A huge screen played a video of Gates, dwarfing Jobs on stage. The audience gasped when they saw the man whom Apple and Jobs had accused of copying the Mac's

OS. According to an article in the *Seattle Times*, Gates said in the video, "We think Apple makes a huge contribution in the computer industry. And we think it's going to be a lot of fun helping out." To ease the crowd's worry, Jobs said, "We have to let go of a few notions here. We have to let go of the notion that for Apple to win, Microsoft needs to lose."

With the deal, Microsoft got to seem a little less like the bad guy of the computer world, and Apple got a much-needed injection of money. Microsoft promised to keep making its popular Microsoft Office software compatible with the Mac, and Apple promised to use Microsoft's Internet browser, Internet Explorer, as the default on its computers (while still offering rival browser Netscape). At the time shocking, the agreement made sense for Apple's financial security.

THE MAC MEETS THE INTERNET

In the early 1990s, the Internet was just beginning to come into public use. Most personal computers were not able to access this means of communication easily. Jobs was interested in bringing an Apple product to the public that could help them access the Web. Unlike his previous projects, Jobs kept this one quiet. There were no pronouncements of how "insanely great" or "revolutionary" this new Apple computer would be.

In May 1998, the iMac was introduced. Its name stood for "Internet Macintosh." It was a stylish Steve Jobs machine: a colorful, see-through plastic case hid the cables, ports, and jacks that made other computers seem complicated. However, unlike Jobs's other products, he managed to balance good design, quality parts, and low price with great results. The iMac was an affordable $1,299. Like the Mac, the user just needed to plug it in. By the end of 1998, Apple sold eight hundred thousand iMacs, making it the fastest-selling personal computer in history. Many iMac users were first-time Apple buyers. Jobs seemed to be making his original dreams for Apple come true. As an added bonus, the company began turning a profit again.

Apple's desktop computers were becoming more powerful. The Power Macintosh released in 1999 had a processor called a G4. It was so fast that it was classified as

The iMac, released in 1998, was the first of the "i" Apple products. It was Jobs's first success after rejoining Apple, and it energized a company that many thought was dying.

a weapon by the U.S. government! Laptop computers such as the PowerBook and, later, the MacBook, made personal computing easier than ever. Each model was slimmer, more stylish, and more powerful than the one before. The products changed with new available technology, incorporating DVD players and wireless Internet capability.

PIXAR FINDS A HOME

Meanwhile, back at Pixar, with the success of *Toy Story*, Jobs wanted a better contract with Disney. Katzenberg had left Disney, and Jobs found himself dealing with the CEO, Michael Eisner. Jobs demanded that Pixar, which was under contract for two more movies, be given half the profits—or it would work with another movie studio after the contract was up. Eisner put up a fight but agreed as long as Pixar made five movies with Disney. (Sequels would not count as part of the five.) Jobs agreed in 1997. His Pixar artists proved again and again that they knew what they were doing with *A Bug's Life* (1998), *Toy Story 2* (1999), *Monsters Inc.* (2001), *Finding Nemo* (2003), *The Incredibles* (2004), and *Cars* (2006).

The contract fulfilled, Jobs again went to Eisner for a new agreement. This time, he wanted Pixar to reap over 90 percent of the profits. Eisner would not budge this far. Jobs threatened to look for another partnership. However, while Disney's other ventures were flagging, Pixar

Steve Jobs holds an iBook, a laptop computer introduced in 1999 that was influenced by the design of the iMac. It was nicknamed "the clamshell" because of its shape.

movies were guaranteed winners. Eventually, Eisner stepped down from his position, pressured to do so after losing his company's confidence.

In 2006, new Disney CEO Robert Iger arranged to buy Pixar for $7.4 billion with the understanding that Pixar would keep its own identity. Jobs would sit on Disney's board of directors and become its largest shareholder. Pixar, now with its money troubles behind it, went on to make *Wall-E* (2008), *Up* (2009), and *Toy Story 3* (2010), among other movies. *Toy Story 3* was the highest-grossing animated film ever.

CHAPTER 7

The Always Innovating Apple Inc.

Apple had a popular ad campaign in the late 1990s. It encouraged people to "Think Different," and it featured black-and-white photos of true visionaries such as Albert Einstein, Thomas Edison, Amelia Earhart, and Jim Henson. The campaign helped create a feeling that Apple was the company for those unafraid to go against the grain. "Think Different" became a slogan for the company's employees as well. Jobs encouraged his team to think differently about new avenues of business.

One way Apple did this was by launching retail stores, starting in 2001. A rare move for a computer company, it was part of an effort to convince Windows PC users to try Macs. Jobs reasoned that they might be more willing to make the switch if they could stop at a store to try one out. One hundred Apple stores opened in the next four years, and all were profitable.

A billboard in Los Angeles, California, features John Lennon and Yoko Ono as figures in Apple's popular "Think Different" ad campaign.

In 2005, Apple did something else that would make Macs even more accessible to PC users. It announced the discontinuation of IBM processors and the beginning of a new venture with Intel. Intel processors were used in Windows PCs, and many thought they were more efficient than the IBM processors of Apple products. As a guarantee to those who wanted to try out a Mac, Apple created a product called Boot Camp that would "boot out" Apple's Mac OS X (a regeneration of the OpenStep operating system), replacing it with Windows if the user needed it.

THE TOOL BUILDER

Jobs thought that the desktop computer wars were coming to an end. Apple would continue to hold a small but loyal share of the computer market, but there were other products that it could excel in. Jobs told Jeff Goodell of *Rolling Stone*, "I'm a tool builder. That's how I think of myself. I want to build really good tools that I know in my gut and my heart will be valuable."

In 2001, Apple announced the iPod. This pocket-sized music player could hold one thousand songs in a digital format. It was not the first portable digital audio device, but like most Apple products, it was an improvement on the existing models. It was sleek with minimal buttons and had exceptional sound quality. The iPod worked with Apple's new software, iTunes, which converted users' CD music into MP3 files so that they could store their music digitally.

Jobs wanted to turn iTunes into a music store as well, but first he needed to persuade record companies to sell their music through this venue. With their agreement, the iTunes Store opened on April 28, 2003. Apple received a portion of every purchase. According to Greg Kot, author of *Ripped: How the Wired Generation Revolutionized Music*, more than one million songs sold at 99 cents apiece in the first week. Jobs had not even made the decision to make iPods and iTunes compatible with other PCs yet. By October 2003, one million iPods had been sold.

Pedestrians pass an eye-catching "Silhouette" ad for the iPod on the side of a building in New York City. Besides music, later generations of iPods could store photos, videos, games, and more.

In 2008, iTunes became the leading music retailer, while many traditional music stores were closing their doors. Other digital music stores, such as Amazon, were gaining a small foothold in the market. New versions of the iPod continued to come out each year, such as the smaller Nano and the inexpensive Shuffle. "There are sneakers that cost more than an iPod," said Jobs in a 2003 interview with *Newsweek*. The digital age had arrived, and Apple had reinvented the music business.

Music Piracy

The digitization of music created a problem. According to Greg Kot's book *Ripped*, Jobs estimated that only about 3 percent of the music in iPods in 2008 was purchased through iTunes. The rest was obtained in other ways, legally converted from people's personal CD collections or illegally downloaded or shared by people on the Internet. For every Internet site that was shut down for allowing people to trade music, two more popped up in its place. Many record companies agreed to participate in the iTunes Store in part because there was little choice. People were distributing digital music illegally; a digital music store was at least a legal and moneymaking alternative.

When the rock band Metallica sued the Internet company Napster in 2000 for encouraging its users to trade copyrighted songs through its servers, many Metallica fans disapproved. They accused the band of being greedy and supporting the record companies, rather than their fans.

Some bands have become creative about dealing with digital music distribution. Radiohead separated from their record company and released their 2007 album *In Rainbows* digitally, allowing fans to pay whatever they wanted for it. The band reported that they made more money doing that than they did for their previous album, which had been released traditionally through a record company. For every album that an artist releases, a percentage goes to the record company, a percentage to the artist, and a percentage to the store. By bypassing the record label and the store, Radiohead made a greater profit.

HEALTH ISSUES

Amid the frenzy of activity at Apple, a 2003 routine medical checkup led to a frightening discovery: a cancerous tumor was found on Jobs's pancreas. A year later in his address at Stanford University, Jobs described the experience of being diagnosed with a deadly form of cancer:

> My doctor advised me to go home and get my affairs in order, which is doctor's code for 'prepare to die.' It means to try to tell your kids everything you thought you'd have the next ten years to tell them in just a few months. It means to make sure everything is buttoned up so that it will be as easy as possible for your family. It means to say your good-byes.

However, a test revealed that the pancreatic cancer was a very rare form and could be treated successfully with surgery. According to a 2008 article in *Fortune* magazine, Jobs tried to treat the cancer with a special diet for nine months before finally agreeing to the procedure. He kept his disease a secret until after the surgery in 2004. He returned to work a mere four weeks later and assured everyone that he was ready to hold the reins of Apple once again.

THE REVOLUTION CONTINUES

At the 2007 Macworld Expo in San Francisco, Jobs said, "This is a day I've been looking forward to for two-and-a-half years." He was speaking of the unveiling of a product that had been so confidential, many Apple engineers had not even known about it. In a 2007 interview with *Fortune*, Phil Schiller—then Apple's head of marketing—said he had to keep the product a secret even from his wife and children. As he left home for the unveiling, Schiller said his son asked, "Dad, can you finally tell us now what you've been working on?" The clandestine product was the iPhone. This mobile cellular device not only made calls; it also surfed the Web.

In a demonstration, Jobs used a Google Web search application to find the nearest Starbucks coffee shop. Then he called it—and ordered four thousand lattes to go! Jobs the showman proclaimed the "revolutionary" product to be five years ahead of any similar product. The iPhone's applications were accessed with a touch of a finger to the

Steve Jobs discusses the iPhone at the 2007 Macworld Expo in front of a giant image of the device's touch screen. The product was an instant sensation.

small screen. It could download movies, music, and videos, and it could share with a Mac or PC such data as contacts, calendars, photos, notes, bookmarks, and e-mails. It could even take photos. And it was as sleek—less than a half-inch (1.27 centimeters) thick—and stylish as any Apple product.

Just seventy-four days after the iPhone was released, the company announced it had sold one million units. A similar-looking 2007 product, the iPod Touch, did everything the iPhone did except make calls. It was the first iPod device to wirelessly connect to the iTunes Store. In 2007, Apple entered another new market with Apple TV, a device that allowed users to play their favorite computer content wirelessly on their televisions, including movies, television shows, music, photos, and podcasts.

Jobs made another announcement at the 2007 expo. Apple Computer was now Apple Inc. The name change signaled Apple's interest in aspects of technology other than just traditional computers, and it was a promise that it would stay on the leading edge of the next big thing.

The next innovation, a tablet computer, was something that Jobs and his crew had actually been working on before the iPhone. At the D8 Conference in 2010, Jobs told the audience what happened when he had the idea of getting rid of the traditional computer keyboard:

> I asked our folks, "Could we come up with a multi-touch display that I could rest my hands on, and

actually type on?" And about six months later, they called me in and showed me this prototype display. And it was amazing. This is in the early 2000s... Now we were thinking about building a phone at that time, and when I saw the rubber band, inertial scrolling, and a few of the other things, I thought, "My God, we could build a phone out of this." And I put the tablet project on the shelf.

After the iPhone was developed, Jobs came back to the project. He introduced the iPad in 2010. Some people dismissed it as a larger iPod Touch. It had the same applications but a larger screen suitable for reading e-books. The consumers did not dismiss it, though, buying two million iPads in two months. The thinner, lighter iPad 2 of 2011 had cameras on the front and back and sold briskly.

A couple of years before the iPad's release, Jobs had said that he believed the personal computer would be phased out as the years went by. It seemed as if tools such as the iPad might make his musings more of a reality. However,

A glass structure in Shanghai, China, ushers shoppers into the underground Apple retail store by way of a spiral staircase.

Apple has not abandoned its PC users. Products like the diminutive Mac Mini hard drive continue to be an attractive alternative to the bulky tower alternatives on the market.

NOT AN OPTION

Everything seemed bright for Apple in 2007, but there were some clouds on the horizon. Beginning in 2006, the U.S. Securities and Exchange Commission (SEC) investigated the practice of backdating stocks at Apple. This meant that stocks were offered to employees, including

Hundreds of excited people lined up outside Apple stores awaiting the release of the iPad. A triumphant customer waves his iPad on April 3, 2010, in New York.

Jobs, at the lower price of a previous date. While Jobs had only been drawing his $1 salary each year as CEO, he had millions of dollars in stock. Questions arose about how much he knew about this practice. He has said that he never benefited, but he did approve of the practice for other employees as a way to keep them from being lured away by other companies.

By 2008, two Apple employees were ordered to compensate the federal government and pay a fine. Jobs was cleared of blame for being unaware of the implications of backdating, a widely known practice among many corporations at the time. In addition, the SEC praised Apple for its cooperation and efforts to prevent such fraudulent activities from happening again.

CONTINUING CONCERNS

Jobs's public appearances in 2008 sparked more rumors about his health. He appeared gaunt, having lost a lot of weight. His spokeswoman told reporters that he had a common bug. In August, the Bloomberg news service mistakenly released Jobs's obituary. A month later, he good-naturedly appeared at a conference, speaking in front of a screen featuring a Mark Twain quote: "The reports of my death have been greatly exaggerated." However, later that year it was announced that Jobs would not deliver the keynote speech at the 2009 Macworld Expo, causing more concern.

In January 2009, Jobs announced that he had a hormonal imbalance that could be treated through nutrition. Just nine days later, he reported that his health issues were more serious than he had thought and that he was handing over Apple's day-to-day operations to Chief Operating Officer Tim Cook. In June, Jobs received a liver transplant. The hospital at which the operation took place released a statement as reported by *ABC News*: "[Jobs] received a liver transplant because he was the patient with the highest MELD score (Model for End-Stage Liver Disease) of his blood type and,

therefore, the sickest patient on the waiting list at the time a donor organ became available." Yet Jobs was back at work just a few weeks later and said he felt great.

In January 2011, Jobs again announced a medical leave of absence, but he did not specify a reason beyond focusing on his health. He said, "I will continue as CEO and be involved in major strategic decisions for the company."

At the unveiling of iCloud in June 2011, Steve Jobs addressed the storage issue for those with multiple Apple devices: "iCloud keeps your important information and content up to date across all your devices . . . you don't even need to think about it—it all just works."

THE "DAY HAS COME"

Jobs appeared at the June 2011 Worldwide Developers Conference (WWDC). He walked in as the James Brown song "I Feel Good" blared from the sound system. He then touted the powers of the new Apple operating system, Lion. He also introduced iCloud, a product that would let people store music, photos, applications, calendars, and documents outside their computers and wirelessly sync the data across multiple devices. It seemed that Jobs's health was not slowing him or the company down. Then, on August 24, 2011, he made an announcement:

> To the Apple Board of Directors and the Apple Community:
>
> I have always said if there ever came a day when I could no longer meet my duties and expectations as Apple's CEO, I would be the first to let you know. Unfortunately, that day has come. I hereby resign as CEO of Apple. I would like to serve, if the Board sees fit, as Chairman of the Board, director, and Apple employee.
>
> As far as my successor goes, I strongly recommend that we execute our succession plan and name Tim Cook as CEO of Apple. I believe Apple's brightest and most innovative days are ahead of it. And I look forward to watching and contributing to its success in a new role.
>
> I have made some of the best friends of my life at Apple, and I thank you all for the many years of being able to work alongside you.
>
> – Steve

Steve Jobs
1955-2011

Upon hearing of Jobs's death in 2011, admirers created tributes in front of Apple stores across the nation, including this one in Boston, Massachusetts.

The news shook the world, topping reports of a rare East Coast earthquake. Apple's stock prices dipped but then recovered. Cook had taken the reins of Apple before, and the transition of leadership had been smooth. The Apple culture that had formed under Jobs's tenure as CEO seemed resilient.

It got its greatest test a little more than a month later, on a day that people feared would come ever since Jobs's announcement in August. Jobs died at home on October 5, 2011, surrounded by loved ones. Despite this tremendous loss, Apple's stock held steady, proving shareholders' confidence in the company and its hand-picked new leader. The public's overwhelming reaction to the news of Jobs's death was as fervent—if not more so—as on the day Jobs stepped down as CEO. Many echoed the statement that appeared on the company's Web site: "Apple has lost a visionary and creative genius, and the world has lost an amazing human being."

Steve Jobs steered Apple as it became the most successful hardware and software producer in the world. He set out to change the world, and few could argue that he didn't. Along the way, he endured failures and basked in the triumphs of beloved projects. He knew he was fortunate. In an interview with *Businessweek*, Jobs put it simply: "I love my family, and I love running Apple, and I love Pixar. And I get to do that. I'm very lucky." Jobs's legacy of leadership and "insanely great" ideas will likely guide Apple for years to come.

Fact Sheet on

STEVE JOBS

Birthplace: San Francisco, California

Born: February 24, 1955

Died: October 5, 2011

College Attended: One semester at Reed College in Portland, Oregon

Marital Status: Married Laurene Powell Jobs

Children: Lisa, Reed, Erin, and Eve

Work Experience: Atari (1974 to 1976)
Apple Computer (1976 to 1985)
NeXT, Inc. (1985 to 1996)
Pixar Animation Studios (1986 to 2011)
The Walt Disney Company (2006 to 2011)
Apple (1996 to 2011)

Number of Shares of Disney Stock: 138 million

Annual Salary at Apple: $1

Number of Shares of Apple Stock: 5.426 million

Net Worth: $8.3 billion

Number on *Forbes* Magazine's 2011 List of Wealthiest People in the United States: 34; In the World: 110

Number of Patents Held: 313

Music on His iPod: Bob Dylan, Beatles, Joan Baez, Rolling Stones, and Yo-Yo Ma

Book on His iPad 2: *The Autobiography of a Yogi* by Paramahansa Yogananda

Quotes from Steve Jobs:

"Innovation has nothing to do with how many R&D [research and development] dollars you have. When Apple came up with the Mac, IBM was spending at least one hundred times more on R&D. It's not about money. It's about the people you have, how you're led, and how much you get it."
— *Fortune*, November 9, 1998

"I didn't see it then, but it turned out that getting fired from Apple was the best thing that could have ever happened to me. The heaviness of being successful was replaced by the lightness of being a beginner again, less sure about everything. It freed me to enter one of the most creative periods of my life."
— Stanford University commencement address, June 2005

"Stay hungry. Stay foolish."
—Stanford University commencement address, June 2005 (quoted from *The Whole Earth Catalog*)

Fact Sheet on

APPLE INC.

Year Founded: 1976

Founders: Steve Jobs, Steve Wozniak, and Ronald Wayne

Headquarters: Cupertino, California

Date Company Became Public: December 1980

CEO: Tim Cook

Stock Symbol: AAPL

First Slogan: "Byte into an Apple."

Net Income (2011): $25,922,000,000

Net Sales (2011): $108,249,000,000

Total Assets (2011): $116,371,000,000

Number of Employees: 46,600 full-time; 2,800 tempo-
rary and contractors

Number of Retail Stores: Nearly 350 locations worldwide

Desktop Computers: iMac, Mac Pro, and Mac Mini

Laptop Computers: MacBook, MacBook Pro, and Mac-
Book Air

Devices: iPhone, iPod, iPad, and Apple TV

Operating System Software: Mac OS X, iOS

Application Software: iLife (featuring iPhoto, iMovie, iDVD, GarageBand, and iWeb); iWord (featuring Pages for word processing and page layout, Keynote for presentations, and Numbers for spreadsheets)

Countries That Manufacture or Assemble Apple Components: United States, China, Czech Republic, Germany, Ireland, Israel, Japan, Korea, Malaysia, Netherlands, Philippines, Taiwan, Thailand, and Singapore

Number of Macs Sold in 2011: 16,735,000

Number of iPhones Sold in 2011: 72,293,000

Number of iPads Sold in 2011: 32,394,000

Number of iPods Sold in 2011: 42,620,000

Timeline

1955 Stephen Paul Jobs is born February 25 in San Francisco, California.

1960 The Jobs family moves to Silicon Valley.

1968 Jobs begins high school and meets Steve Wozniak.

1973 Jobs attends Reed College for one semester and drops out.

1974 Jobs works at Atari designing video games.

1976 Jobs and Wozniak found Apple Computer, with the release of Apple I.

1977 Apple II is unveiled to the public and is highly successful.

1978 Jobs's first daughter, Lisa, is born.

1979 Jobs visits Xerox PARC, where he is introduced to the graphical user interface.

1980 Apple III is released with poor results; Apple Computer becomes a publicly traded company.

1983 The Lisa is released with a GUI but performs poorly in the market; Apple's Kids Can't Wait program donates computers to about ten thousand California schools.

1984 The Macintosh is released; initial sales are slow.

1985 Steve Wozniak leaves Apple; Jobs resigns from Apple and begins NeXT Computer, Inc.

1986 The Mac Plus becomes a huge success; Jobs buys Pixar from George Lucas.

1988 The Pixar Image Computer II is released; the NeXT Computer System is released.

1991 Jobs marries Laurene Powell and she gives birth to their first son, Reed; Jobs shuts down Pixar hardware operations; the Pixar animation team makes a deal with Disney.

1993 Jobs lays off three hundred employees at NeXT and refocuses it as a software company.

1995 Pixar and Disney release *Toy Story*; Pixar goes public with Jobs as CEO; Jobs's daughter Erin Sienna is born.

1996 Apple agrees to buy NeXT.

1997 Jobs becomes the interim CEO of Apple; he makes a deal with Microsoft.

1998 iMac is introduced and becomes the fastest-selling Mac; Jobs's daughter Eve is born.

2000 Jobs becomes the permanent CEO of Apple.

2001 Apple releases the iPod music player; it opens its first retail stores: the first two locations are in McLean, Virginia, and Glendale, California.

2003 The iTunes Store opens; Jobs is diagnosed with pancreatic cancer.

2006 Disney buys Pixar, and Jobs becomes largest Disney shareholder; he introduces Macs with Intel processors.

2007 Apple Computer releases the hugely successful iPhone and changes its name to Apple Inc.

2009 Jobs takes time off from the company for health concerns.

2010 Jobs introduces the iPad tablet.

2011 Apple surpasses Exxon Mobil as the most valuable U.S. company in August; Jobs resigns as CEO of Apple and Tim Cook becomes the company's chief executive.

2011 Jobs dies on October 5.

Glossary

application A computer program or piece of software designed to perform a specific task.

automated Using mechanical or electronic devices with little or no human labor required.

BASIC An early programming language that is still among the simplest and most popular; stands for "Beginner's All-Purpose Symbolic Instruction Code."

byte A unit of computer memory.

capital Money or other resources used to produce further wealth.

charisma The ability to inspire enthusiasm, interest, or affection in others by means of personal charm.

circuit board A flat, multilayered board that holds microchips and circuits that are interconnected via copper pathways.

clandestine Held or done in secrecy.

commune A community in which possessions and responsibilities are shared.

configuration The way in which the software and hardware components of a computer system are arranged and connected so that the systems function correctly.

default A selection automatically used by a computer program or device when the user does not specify a choice.

digital Relating to information stored using a series of ones and zeros. Computers are digital machines because they can only read information as on or off—1 or 0.

graphical user interface (GUI) A way for people to interact with a computer that relies on icons, windows, menus, and a mouse or touchpad, rather than typing in commands.

guru An intellectual or spiritual guide.

iconic Relating to someone or something that is greatly admired.

inertial scrolling The ability of a trackpad or touch screen to sense the momentum of a person's finger gestures and translate that into the speed of page scrolling.

integrated circuit A small group of electronic components contained within a single chip, usually made of silicon, with many functions, such as performing calculations and storing data.

interim Serving temporarily until a permanent replacement can be appointed.

intuitive Capable of being known directly and instinctively.

kilobyte A unit of computer memory equal to 1,024 bytes.

license To give official permission for somebody to do something or for an activity to take place.

microprocessor The central processing unit that performs the basic operations in a microcomputer.

It consists of an integrated circuit contained on a single chip.

MP3 A computer file format for the compression of digital audio; stands for "MPEG-1 Audio Layer III."

operating system The essential program in a computer that maintains disk files, runs applications, and manages devices such as the keyboard, mouse, monitor, and printer.

optical disk A rigid computer storage disk on which data is stored as tiny pits in the plastic coating and which is readable by laser.

port An external socket on a computer's central processing unit where an external device such as a printer, keyboard, or network cable is plugged in.

programming language A vocabulary and set of rules for writing computer programs.

random access memory (RAM) The main memory that is internal to the computer and available to run programs and store data.

sans serif A style of typeface in which there are no decorative lines.

serif A short decorative line at the start or finish of a stroke in a letter.

share An equal, usually small, part of a company's stock.

silicon An abundant, brittle, nonmetallic chemical element found in nature. It is used as the semiconductor base on which an integrated circuit is laid out for computer chips.

sync To merge or update the data between a device and a computer; short for "synchronize."

Teletype A communication device similar to a typewriter used for data input and output; also called a teletypewriter.

typeface A style of printed character, such as bold or Times New Roman.

ubiquitous Existing everywhere at once; constantly encountered.

venture capital Money used for investment in new businesses that involve high risk but offer the possibility of large profits.

visionary One who has a powerful imagination and unusual foresight.

Apple Canada

7495 Birchmount Road

Markham, ON L3R 5G2

Canada

(905) 513-5800

Web site: http://www.apple.com/ca

Apple Inc.'s Canadian Web site has links to product information, as well as links to technical support and the nearest Apple retail stores.

Apple Inc.

1 Infinite Loop

Cupertino, CA 95014

(408) 996-1010

Web site: http://www.apple.com

Apple Inc. is a designer, manufacturer, and marketer of a wide range of personal computers, mobile communication devices, and portable digital music players.

Apples BC Computer Society

258 - 3495 Cambie Street

Vancouver, BC V5Z 4R3

Canada

(778) 385-7440

Web site: http://web.mac.com/applesbc/applesbc/ApplesBC.html

Apples BC Computer Society is a Vancouver, Canada–based group dedicated to helping people get the most out of their Macintosh and other Apple Inc. and compatible products.

Atlanta Macintosh Users Group (AMUG)

P.O. Box 15130

Atlanta, GA 30333-0130

(678) 408-AMUG [2684]

Web site: http://amugonline.org

Founded in 1984, the AMUG is organized for the purpose of providing education and assistance to its members in the use of the Apple Macintosh computer and software.

Macworld

P.O. Box 37781

Boone, IA 50037-0781

(800) 288-6848

Web site: http://www.macworld.com

Macworld is a Web site with a companion magazine that provides news, reviews, help, and forums for Mac enthusiasts.

Pixar Animation Studios

1200 Park Avenue

Emeryville, CA 94608

(510) 922-3000

Web site: http://www.pixar.com

Pixar is the animation studio behind *Toy Story, Finding Nemo*, and *Monsters Inc.*, among others. In 2006, it became a wholly owned subsidary of the Walt Disney Company.

WEB SITES

Due to the changing nature of Internet links, Rosen Publishing has developed an online list of Web sites related to the subject of this book. This site is updated regularly. Please use this link to access the list:

http://www.rosenlinks.com/ibio/jobs

Buckley, A. M. *Pixar: The Company and Its Founders* (Technology Pioneers). Edina, MN: ABDO Publishing, 2011.

Corrigan, Jim. *Business Leaders: Steve Jobs*. Greensboro, NC: Morgan Reynolds Publishing, 2009.

Elliot, Jay, and William L. Simon. *The Steve Jobs Way: iLeadership for a New Generation*. New York, NY: Vanguard Press, 2011.

Gallo, Carmine. *The Innovation Secrets of Steve Jobs: Insanely Different: Principles for Breakthrough Success*. New York, NY: McGraw-Hill, 2011.

Gilbert, Sara. *The Story of Apple* (Built for Success). Mankato, MN: Creative Education, 2011.

Gilliam, Scott. *Steve Jobs: Apple & iPod Wizard* (Essential Lives). Edina, MN: ABDO Publishing, 2008.

Goldsmith, Mike, and Tom Jackson. *Computer*. New York, NY: DK Publishing, 2011.

Goldsworthy, Steve. *Steve Jobs* (Remarkable People). New York, NY: AV2 by Weigl, 2011.

Imbimbo, Anthony. *Steve Jobs: The Brilliant Mind Behind Apple* (Life Portraits). Pleasantville, NY: Gareth Stevens Publishing, 2009.

Kahney, Leander. *Inside Steve's Brain*. New York, NY: Portfolio, 2008.

Lemke, Donald B. *Steve Jobs, Steve Wozniak, and the Personal Computer* (Graphic Library). Mankato, MN: Capstone Press, 2007.

Levy, Steven. *The Perfect Thing: How the iPod Shuffles Commerce, Culture, and Coolness*. New York, NY: Simon & Schuster, 2006.

Lohr, Steve. *Digital Revolutionaries: The Men and Women Who Brought Computers to Life*. New York, NY: Rb Flash Point, 2009.

Moritz, Michael. *Return to the Little Kingdom: Steve Jobs, The Creation of Apple, and How It Changed the World*. New York, NY: Overlook Press, 2009.

O'Grady, Jason D. *Apple Inc.* (Corporations That Changed the World). Westport, CT: Greenwood Press, 2009.

Sheen, Barbara. *Steve Jobs* (People in the News). Detroit, MI: Lucent Books, 2010.

Sutherland, Adam. *The Story of Apple* (The Business of High Tech). New York, NY: Rosen Central, 2012.

Venezia, Mike. *Steve Jobs & Steve Wozniak: Geek Heroes Who Put the Personal in Computers*. New York, NY: Children's Press, 2010.

Wozniak, Steve, and Gina Smith. *IWoz: Computer Geek to Cult Icon: How I Invented the Personal Computer, Co-Founded Apple, and Had Fun Doing It*. New York, NY: W. W. Norton & Co., 2006.

Bibliography

Appleyard, Bryan. "Steve Jobs: The Man Who Polished Apple." *Sunday Times*, August 16, 2009. Retrieved July 23, 2011 (http://technology.timesonline.co.uk/tol/news/tech_and_web/article6797859.ece).

Bloomberg News. "Steve Jobs's Health Reports Since His Cancer Diagnosis in 2003: Timeline." January 17, 2011. Retrieved August 13, 2011 (http://www.bloomberg.com/news/2011-01-17/steve-jobs-s-health-reports-since-his-cancer-diagnosis-in-2003-timeline.html).

Burrows, Peter. "The Seed of Apple's Innovation." *Businessweek*, October 12, 2004. Retrieved August 2, 2011 (www.businessweek.com/bwdaily/dnflash/oct2004/nf20041012_4018_db083.htm).

Cocks, Jay. "The Updated Book Off Jobs." *TIME*, January 3, 1983. Retrieved August 5, 2011 (http://www.time.com/time/magazine/article/0,9171,953633,00.html).

Elkind, Peter. "The Trouble with Steve Jobs." *Fortune*, March 5, 2008. Retrieved August 1, 2011 (http://money.cnn.com/2008/03/02/news/companies/elkind_jobs.fortune/index.htm).

Foljanty, Lukas. "2000–Present: The iPod Era." Apple Museum, 2010. Retrieved August 13, 2011 (http://www.theapplemuseum.com/index.php?id=58).

FOXNews.com. "Apple's Jobs Takes Stage to Unveil iCloud Music Service." June 6, 2011. Retrieved August 13, 2011 (http://www.foxnews.com/scitech/2011/06/06/apples-jobs-takes-stage-unveils-icloud-music-service#ixzz1TvPc0nGX).

Goodell, Jeff. "Steve Jobs in 1994: The *Rolling Stone* Interview." *Rolling Stone*, January 17, 2011. Retrieved August 10, 2011 (http://www.rollingstone.com/culture/news/steve-jobs-in-1994-the-rolling-stone-interview-20110117).

Heussner, Ki Mae, and Dean Schabner. "Hospital Confirms Jobs' Liver Transplant." *ABC News*, June 23, 2009. Retrieved August 10, 2011 (http://abcnews.go.com/Technology/AheadoftheCurve/story?id=7900907).

Hormby, Tom. "Origin of the Apple I and Apple II Computers." May 9, 2005. Retrieved July 15, 2011 (http://lowendmac.com/orchard/05/origin-apple-ii-computer.html).

Jobs, Steve. "Text of Steve Jobs' Commencement Address (2005)." *Stanford Report*, June 14, 2005. Retrieved August 10, 2011 (http://news.stanford.edu/news/2005/june15/jobs-061505.html).

Kot, Greg. *Ripped: How the Wired Generation Revolutionized Music*. New York, NY: Scribner, 2009.

Lewis, Peter H. "How Apple Kept Its iPhone Secrets." *Fortune*, January 12, 2007. Retrieved August 15, 2011 (http://money.cnn.com/2007/01/10/commentary/lewis_fortune_iphone.fortune).

Linzmayer, Owen. *Apple Confidential 2.0: The Definitive History of the World's Most Colorful Company*. Rev. 2nd ed. San Francisco, CA: No Starch Press, 2004.

Linzmayer, Owen, and Bryan Chaffin. "This Week in Apple History—December 12–18: Apple Goes Public, 1984 Airs." Mac Observer, December 16, 2004. Retrieved August 13, 2011 (http://www.macobserver.com/columns/thisweek/2004/20041218.shtml).

Lohr, Steve. "Creating Jobs: Apple's Founder Goes Home Again." *New York Times Magazine*, January 12, 1997. Retrieved June 30, 2011 (http://partners.nytimes.com/library/cyber/week/011897jobs.html).

Matassa Flores, Michele, and Thomas W. Haines. "Microsoft, Apple Join Forces—Disbelief, Boos Greet Today's Stunning Announcement at Macworld Expo." *Seattle Times*, August 6, 1997. Retrieved August 11, 2011 (http://community.seattletimes.nwsource.com/archive/?date=19970806&slug=2553374).

Morrow, Daniel. "Smithsonian Oral and Video Histories: Steve Jobs." Smithsonian Institution, April 20, 1995.

Retrieved July 14, 2011 (http://americanhistory. si.edu/collections/comphist/sj1.html).

Ortutay, Barbara. "iPads Trump Oil: Apple Is Most Valuable US Company." Associated Press, August 11, 2011. Retrieved August 13, 2011 (http://news.yahoo. com/ipads-trump-oil-apple-most-valuable-us-company-230040347.html).

PBS.org. "Triumph of the Nerds: The Transcripts: Part III." Retrieved August 14, 2011 (http://www.pbs.org/ nerds/part3.html).

Price, David A. *The Pixar Touch: The Making of a Company*. New York, NY: Alfred A. Knopf, 2008.

Stross, Randall E. *Steve Jobs and the NeXT Big Thing*. New York, NY: Atheneum, 1993.

Wozniak, Steve. "How We Failed Apple: A Founder Laments a Legendary Company's Decline." *Newsweek*, February 19, 1996. Retrieved August 5, 2011 (http:// woz.com/pages/wozscape/Articles/Newsweek_ FailingApple/FailingApple.HTML).

YouTube.com. "Apple Shareholder Meeting 1984—The First Macintosh." Retrieved July 23, 2011 (http://www. youtube.com/watch?v=zJ12vNZ5yMY).

Index

ABOUT THE AUTHOR

Therese Shea, an author and former educator, has written more than one hundred books on a wide variety of subjects, most recently robotics. She holds degrees from Providence College and the State University of New York at Buffalo. An enthusiast of all things Apple, she enjoyed delving into the behind-the-scenes stories of some of her favorite devices. The author currently resides in Atlanta, Georgia, with her husband, Mark.

PHOTO CREDITS

Designer: Brian Garvey; Editor: Andrea Sclarow Paskoff; Photo Researcher: Marty Levick